W9-AGE-149

MAD LIBS JUNIOR

SPORTS STAR
MAD LIBS JUNIOR

By Roger Price and Leonard Stern

Mad Libs
An Imprint of Penguin Random House

MAD LIBS
An Imprint of Penguin Random House LLC, New York

Mad Libs format and text copyright © 2004 by Penguin Random House LLC. All rights reserved.

Concept created by Roger Price & Leonard Stern

Published by Mad Libs,
an imprint of Penguin Random House LLC, New York.
Printed in the USA.

Visit us online at www.penguinrandomhouse.com.

Penguin supports copyright. Copyright fuels creativity, encourages diverse voices, promotes free speech, and creates a vibrant culture. Thank you for buying an authorized edition of this book and for complying with copyright laws by not reproducing, scanning, or distributing any part of it in any form without permission. You are supporting writers and allowing Penguin to continue to publish books for every reader.

ISBN 9780843107708
21

MAD LIBS and MAD LIBS JUNIOR are registered trademarks of Penguin Random House LLC.

MAD LIBS JUNIOR® is a game for kids who don't like games!
It can be played by one, two, three, four, or forty.

RIDICULOUSLY SIMPLE DIRECTIONS:

At the top of each page in this book, you will find four columns of words, each headed by a symbol. Each symbol represents a part of speech. The symbols are:

★	⊙	➜	?
NOUNS	ADJECTIVES	VERBS	MISC.

MAD LIBS JUNIOR® is fun to play with friends, but you can also play it by yourself! To begin, look at the story on the page below. When you come to a blank space in the story, look at the symbol that appears underneath. Then find the same symbol on this page and pick a word that appears below the symbol. Put that word in the blank space, and cross out the word, so you don't use it again. Continue doing this throughout the story until you've filled in all the spaces. Finally, read your story aloud and laugh!

EXAMPLE:

"Good-bye!" he said, as he jumped into his _____ and _____
                                ?   ➜

off with his pet _____ .
            ★

★	⊙	➜	?
NOUNS	ADJECTIVES	VERBS	MISC.
hamster	curly	drove	car
dog	purple	~~danced~~	boat
cat	wet	drank	roller skate
~~giraffe~~	tired	twirled	taxicab
monkey	silly	swam	~~surfboard~~

"Good-bye!" he said, as he jumped into his _____SURFBOARD_____ and _____DANCED_____
                                ?   ➜

off with his pet _____GIRAFFE_____ .
            ★

In case you haven't learned about the parts of speech yet, here is a quick lesson:

A **NOUN** ✦ is the name of a person, place, or thing. *Sidewalk, umbrella, bathtub,* and *roller blades* are nouns.

An **ADJECTIVE** ☺ describes a person, place, or thing. *Lumpy, soft, ugly, messy,* and *short* are adjectives.

A **VERB** ➔ is an action word. *Run, jump,* and *swim* are verbs.

MISC. ? will be any word that does not apply to the other categories. Some examples of a word that could be miscellaneous are: *part of the body, animal, number, color*, and *a place*.

MAD LIBS JUNIOR® is fun to play with friends, but you can also play it by yourself! To begin, look at the story on the page below. When you come to a blank space in the story, look at the symbol that appears underneath. Then find the same symbol on this page and pick a word that appears below the symbol. Put that word in the blank space, and cross out the word, so you don't use it again. Continue doing this throughout the story until you've filled in all the spaces. Finally, read your story aloud and laugh!

BOWLING BIRTHDAY

★	☺	→	?
NOUNS	**ADJECTIVES**	**VERBS**	**MISC.**
clowns	smelly	cheering	shoes
monkeys	greasy	laughing	helmets
fools	cool	barfing	vests
jellyfish	stinky	singing	hats
monsters	slimy	farting	socks
turkeys	good	crying	shirts
hot dogs	serious	dancing	underwear
snowmen	awesome	shaking	pants
pumpkins	fun	hopping	jeans
grapes	dirty	yelling	bathing suits
poodles	gross	screaming	mittens
cupcakes	nasty	jumping	scarves

MAD LIBS 😊 JUNIOR.
BOWLING BIRTHDAY

For my birthday, my parents took me and my best friends to the

Super _____ Lanes to go bowling. I love the bowling alley—it's

so _____! First, we all rented funny bowling _____ and
?

changed into them. We had to leave our _____ with the front
?

desk. I thought we looked like a bunch of _____. Our lanes were
★

next to a group of people wearing _____ with their names sewn
?

on them. They must have been really _____ bowlers. On my first

try, I started _____, then rolled my ball down the lane. I knocked
→

over all of the _____ at the end of the lane and all my friends
★

started _____. What a/an _____ time we had bowling on
→

my birthday!

From SPORTS STAR MAD LIBS JUNIOR® • Copyright © 2004 by Penguin Random House LLC.

MAD LIBS JUNIOR® is fun to play with friends, but you can also play it by yourself! To begin, look at the story on the page below. When you come to a blank space in the story, look at the symbol that appears underneath. Then find the same symbol on this page and pick a word that appears below the symbol. Put that word in the blank space, and cross out the word, so you don't use it again. Continue doing this throughout the story until you've filled in all the spaces. Finally, read your story aloud and laugh!

TIPS FOR THE PERFECT DIVE

★	☺	➡	?
NOUNS	**ADJECTIVES**	**VERBS**	**MISC.**
banana	tall	burping	sunglasses
octopus	boring	laughing	earmuffs
dolphin	scary	sweating	mittens
submarine	steep	kicking	jeans
elephant	silly	shaking	goggles
pretzel	narrow	barfing	underwear
whale	big	dancing	gloves
noodle	wimpy	crying	pants
donut	nasty	flapping	socks
penguin	crazy	giggling	headphones
candy cane	good	singing	earrings
ostrich	wacky	screaming	shoes

Here are four _____ tips to doing a perfect dive:

Tip 1: Whenever you are diving, wear a good pair of _____.

These will keep the water from getting where it shouldn't.

Tip 2: Stay calm—even if you're going off a really _____

high-dive. If your nerves get the best of you, you may start

_____ and lose your cool.

Tip 3: _____ form is everything. Keep your arms straight

and bend your body like a/an _____.

Tip 4: As soon as you jump off the board, start _____. This

way, you will land in the water just like a/an _____.

From SPORTS STAR MAD LIBS JUNIOR® • Copyright © 2004 by Penguin Random House LLC.

MAD LIBS JUNIOR® is fun to play with friends, but you can also play it by yourself! To begin, look at the story on the page below. When you come to a blank space in the story, look at the symbol that appears underneath. Then find the same symbol on this page and pick a word that appears below the symbol. Put that word in the blank space, and cross out the word, so you don't use it again. Continue doing this throughout the story until you've filled in all the spaces. Finally, read your story aloud and laugh!

FLAG FOOTBALL

★	☺	➡	?
NOUNS	**ADJECTIVES**	**VERBS**	**MISC.**
lizard	funny	kicking	hat
pickle	goofy	dancing	shorts
jellyfish	nasty	singing	shirt
ham	smelly	moving	pants
goat	gross	running	underwear
spaceship	grassy	farting	sweater
pizza	muddy	cheering	sweat suit
toilet	slimy	burping	skirt
lemon	slippery	screaming	helmet
monkey	ugly	laughing	sock
pumpkin	hairy	coughing	overalls
sausage	lumpy	jumping	bathing suit

MAD LIBS JUNIOR.
FLAG FOOTBALL

Sometimes, all the neighborhood kids get together for a/an

_____ game of flag football. Every kid puts on their

_____ _____ and heads over to the

_____ field behind the school. Each player attaches a

_____ to their _____, and the other players try

to pull them off. It really is quite _____! You score points by

catching a _____ and then _____. One time

when we were playing, I tripped on an old _____ and tore

my _____. I felt kind of _____, but I kept on

_____ and scored a point for my team. Then everyone started

_____ and told me what a/an _____

player I was!

From SPORTS STAR MAD LIBS JUNIOR® • Copyright © 2004 by Penguin Random House LLC.

MAD LIBS JUNIOR® is fun to play with friends, but you can also play it by yourself! To begin, look at the story on the page below. When you come to a blank space in the story, look at the symbol that appears underneath. Then find the same symbol on this page and pick a word that appears below the symbol. Put that word in the blank space, and cross out the word, so you don't use it again. Continue doing this throughout the story until you've filled in all the spaces. Finally, read your story aloud and laugh!

AT THE BATTING CAGE

★ NOUNS	☺ ADJECTIVES	➡ VERBS	? MISC.
pickles	best	shakes	socks
rubber bands	worst	dances	caps
sardines	coolest	farts	shirts
peanuts	hottest	sings	shorts
lightbulbs	slimiest	laughs	jerseys
onions	greasiest	burps	gloves
hot dogs	greatest	claps	shoes
chickens	nastiest	cheers	ties
marshmallows	tastiest	jumps	hats
insects	smelliest	wiggles	boots
noodles	silliest	barfs	slippers
French fries	ugliest	sways	belts

One of the _____ things to do in the summer is to go to a

baseball game. My favorite team is the Red _____. My dad

?

and I always wear matching _____ with our favorite player's

?

number on them. He's the _____ player in the lineup. We

always sit along the third-base line and try to catch _____

★

when they fly into the stands. I also love the food at the ballpark—it's the

_____! I could eat _____ and _____ all

★ ★

day long. But I think the _____ part of going to baseball

games is how the whole crowd _____ at once. Everyone

➡

stands up and _____ when they play "Take Me Out to the

➡

Ball Game."

From SPORTS STAR MAD LIBS JUNIOR® • Copyright © 2004 by Penguin Random House LLC.

MAD LIBS JUNIOR® is fun to play with friends, but you can also play it by yourself! To begin, look at the story on the page below. When you come to a blank space in the story, look at the symbol that appears underneath. Then find the same symbol on this page and pick a word that appears below the symbol. Put that word in the blank space, and cross out the word, so you don't use it again. Continue doing this throughout the story until you've filled in all the spaces. Finally, read your story aloud and laugh!

OUR BASKETBALL COACH

★	☺	➡	?
NOUNS	**ADJECTIVES**	**VERBS**	**MISC.**
toad	chubby	dance	tie
toilet	goofy	giggle	sweat suit
pear	nice	cry	jacket
hippo	old	sweat	bathing suit
trash can	ugly	jump	sock
bird	crazy	cheer	shoe
pineapple	wrinkly	scream	scarf
whale	smelly	sing	hat
beetle	funny	run	sweater
tugboat	happy	yell	girdle
lizard	nervous	shake	crown
cow	positive	boogie	T-shirt

MAD LIBS JUNIOR
OUR BASKETBALL COACH

Our basketball coach, Mr. Whipple, is really _____. He likes to

_____ and looks kind of like a _____. He told us

that when he played basketball in school, his nickname was "The

_____" because he was so _____. At our games,

Mr. Whipple always wears a/an _____ _____ for

good luck. If we're playing really badly, his face gets all _____

and he starts to _____. But he's always _____.

Whenever a player comes out of the game he says, "Way to

_____, sport!" At the end of the season, we're going to give

Mr. Whipple a _____ that says, "World's Best Basketball Coach."

From SPORTS STAR MAD LIBS JUNIOR® • Copyright © 2004 by Penguin Random House LLC.

MAD LIBS JUNIOR® is fun to play with friends, but you can also play it by yourself! To begin, look at the story on the page below. When you come to a blank space in the story, look at the symbol that appears underneath. Then find the same symbol on this page and pick a word that appears below the symbol. Put that word in the blank space, and cross out the word, so you don't use it again. Continue doing this throughout the story until you've filled in all the spaces. Finally, read your story aloud and laugh!

WRESTLING STAR

★ NOUNS	😊 ADJECTIVES	→ VERBS	? MISC.
moose	furry	moans	socks
monkey	shiny	yells	boots
monster	glittery	laughs	tights
marshmallow	silky	jumps	earrings
muffin	slimy	burps	shoes
maniac	stinky	giggles	pants
meatball	tight	dances	underwear
moth	super	hops	slippers
mushroom	slippery	farts	mittens
mule	smelly	wiggles	glasses
mouth	stupid	shakes	gloves
maid	silly	spins	shorts

MAD LIBS JUNIOR
WRESTLING STAR

I love to watch wrestling. My favorite wrestling star is Marty the

_____. He wears _____ black-and-white

_____ and a big, red mask. Before every match, Marty comes

out and rips off his _____ and _____ like a

_____. The other night, I saw him beat Spike the

_____ Snake. Whenever Spike _____ in the

ring, the whole crowd starts to boo. Marty grabbed Spike by the

_____ and spun him around. Then he gave him a

_____ kick right in the _____. When it was all

over, Spike looked just like a _____ _____. Then,

Marty won a big, _____ belt. He is so _____!

From SPORTS STAR MAD LIBS JUNIOR® • Copyright © 2004 by Penguin Random House LLC.

MAD LIBS JUNIOR® is fun to play with friends, but you can also play it by yourself! To begin, look at the story on the page below. When you come to a blank space in the story, look at the symbol that appears underneath. Then find the same symbol on this page and pick a word that appears below the symbol. Put that word in the blank space, and cross out the word, so you don't use it again. Continue doing this throughout the story until you've filled in all the spaces. Finally, read your story aloud and laugh!

IN-LINE SKATING

★ NOUNS	☺ ADJECTIVES	→ VERBS	? MISC.
pickle	nasty	dance	bathing suit
corn dog	tasty	skate	helmet
turnip	slimy	scoot	jacket
octopus	silly	shimmy	cap
Popsicle	fuzzy	wiggle	shirt
pizza	gross	creep	shoe
chicken	old	boogie	suit
sardine	lumpy	slither	wig
hamburger	cheesy	squirm	tie
jellyfish	smelly	shake	vest
milkshake	goofy	crawl	helmet
tuna fish	stinky	slide	dress

MAD LIBS JUNIOR.
IN-LINE SKATING

Every Saturday, my friends and I go in-line skating at the

_____ roller rink. They play _____ music there

and have _____-colored lights that flash. I always wear my

purple _____ because it looks so _____.

? Sometimes, they have a limbo contest where you can try to

_____ your way under a pole as they make it lower and

→ lower. My friend won once and got a _____ that said, "I love

? to _____." My favorite is "_____ skate," when I

→ can _____ like a/an _____ while I'm skating. My

→ least favorite part is "couples skate," when you have to skate with a/an

_____. After we skate for a while, we head to the

snack bar for some hot _____ nachos. Mmmmm!

From SPORTS STAR MAD LIBS JUNIOR® • Copyright © 2004 by Penguin Random House LLC.

MAD LIBS JUNIOR® is fun to play with friends, but you can also play it by yourself! To begin, look at the story on the page below. When you come to a blank space in the story, look at the symbol that appears underneath. Then find the same symbol on this page and pick a word that appears below the symbol. Put that word in the blank space, and cross out the word, so you don't use it again. Continue doing this throughout the story until you've filled in all the spaces. Finally, read your story aloud and laugh!

TIPS TO THROWING THE PERFECT CURVEBALL

★	☺	→	?
NOUNS	**ADJECTIVES**	**VERBS**	**MISC.**
egg	slippery	cough	underwear
clam	hot	look	glove
apple	slimy	sneeze	hat
pinecone	lumpy	fart	belt
watermelon	silly	snort	scarf
octopus	funny	laugh	shoe
tissue	dirty	drool	sock
potato	greasy	barf	bracelet
sandwich	smooth	yell	cap
bowling ball	gross	burp	jersey
diaper	soft	breathe	bathing suit
golf club	wet	spit	slipper

These _____ tips will teach you the key to every pitcher's

_____ weapon:

1. First, always make sure your _____ fits securely on

   your hand. If it's loose, it might make you _____.

2. Quickly _____ into your hand and then rub your hand

   gently over the ball until it feels nice and _____.

3. Bring your arm back and lift your leg, until it is level with

   your _____.

4. Throw the ball as if it were a _____ _____.

5. Always _____ as you release the ball. That gives it the

   perfect curve!

From SPORTS STAR MAD LIBS JUNIOR® • Copyright © 2004 by Penguin Random House LLC.

MAD LIBS JUNIOR® is fun to play with friends, but you can also play it by yourself! To begin, look at the story on the page below. When you come to a blank space in the story, look at the symbol that appears underneath. Then find the same symbol on this page and pick a word that appears below the symbol. Put that word in the blank space, and cross out the word, so you don't use it again. Continue doing this throughout the story until you've filled in all the spaces. Finally, read your story aloud and laugh!

SWIM RELAY RACE

★ NOUNS	😊 ADJECTIVES	➡ VERBS	? MISC.
dolphin	grumpy	shake	underwear
chicken	lazy	tickle	goggles
toilet	happy	kick	sunglasses
noodle	sick	poke	gloves
frog	wild	sniff	boots
poodle	wet	hug	slippers
dragon	slippery	punch	socks
wizard	nervous	smell	shoes
alien	excited	lift	suspenders
deer	fat	kiss	earrings
submarine	tired	wiggle	water wings
puppy	crazy	grab	pants

MAD LIBS JUNIOR
SWIM RELAY RACE

At our last swim meet, I swam in our _____ team relay race.

We all put on our _____ and our _____ and

lined up. We waited for the referee to _____ her

_____ to signal the start of the race. My friend Susie was

doing the _____ stroke for the first part of the race. She

jumped into the water like a/an _____ _____

and started to swim. Fred was up next, and he did the _____

paddle so hard his _____ fell off. When I jumped in the water,

I was feeling very _____. I didn't even realize we had won

until I got out of the pool and everyone came up and started to

_____ me!

From SPORTS STAR MAD LIBS JUNIOR® • Copyright © 2004 by Penguin Random House LLC.

MAD LIBS JUNIOR® is fun to play with friends, but you can also play it by yourself! To begin, look at the story on the page below. When you come to a blank space in the story, look at the symbol that appears underneath. Then find the same symbol on this page and pick a word that appears below the symbol. Put that word in the blank space, and cross out the word, so you don't use it again. Continue doing this throughout the story until you've filled in all the spaces. Finally, read your story aloud and laugh!

DODGEBALL

★ NOUNS	☺ ADJECTIVES	→ VERBS	? MISC.
apple	stinky	run	shirt
kangaroo	mean	wiggle	hat
watermelon	nasty	dance	cape
shark	silly	sing	underpants
pumpkin	dumb	skip	shoe
corn	smelly	hop	sock
lobster	crazy	fart	scarf
fish	scary	scamper	shorts
muffin	rotten	leap	jacket
guppy	squishy	shake	eye patch
cake	sick	burp	uniform
snake	wet	jump	belt

MAD LIBS JUNIOR.
DODGEBALL

When my class goes out for recess, we like to play a _____

game called dodgeball. The rules are very _____. You

split up into two groups—some kids go in the middle that we call the

"_____ pit" and the other kids go on the line. The kids

on the line each try to throw a _____ _____

ball at the kids in the middle. You've got to _____ really

quickly to avoid getting hit! If it does hit you, then you have to go

_____ on the line. The other day, this _____ kid

named Stewie, who looks like a/an _____, hit me so hard

my _____ fell off. Dodgeball sure is a _____ game!

From SPORTS STAR MAD LIBS JUNIOR® • Copyright © 2004 by Penguin Random House LLC.

MAD LIBS JUNIOR® is fun to play with friends, but you can also play it by yourself! To begin, look at the story on the page below. When you come to a blank space in the story, look at the symbol that appears underneath. Then find the same symbol on this page and pick a word that appears below the symbol. Put that word in the blank space, and cross out the word, so you don't use it again. Continue doing this throughout the story until you've filled in all the spaces. Finally, read your story aloud and laugh!

FITNESS TEST

★	☺	➡	?
NOUNS	**ADJECTIVES**	**VERBS**	**MISC.**
brick	crazy	hop	socks
whale	wacky	skip	caps
refrigerator	chubby	jump	gym shorts
lion	goofy	crawl	T-shirts
fish tank	silly	run	sweatshirts
elephant	fuzzy	limp	nightgowns
toilet	scrawny	sprint	boots
table	weak	stumble	jackets
house	stupid	tiptoe	sweatbands
cupcake	ugly	slither	pajamas
fiddle	skinny	creep	slippers
hippo	funny	wander	snowsuits

MAD LIBS JUNIOR.
FITNESS TEST

"Okay, class, listen up. Here are the rules for this year's _____

fitness test, which starts tomorrow. Be sure to dress in your

_____ and your _____. Your scores will come

?　　　　　　　　　**?**

from three _____ events. The first is the shuttle run, where

you have to _____ ten yards, then quickly pick up a/an

➡

_____ and run back. The next is the _____ run,

★　　　　　　　　　　　　　　　　　　　　**☺**

where you have to _____ around a/an _____

➡　　　　　　　　　　　　　　　**★**

five times. Finally, you have to do five chin ups, pulling yourself up on a

bar with your _____ arms. If the class scores 95 percent or

☺

higher, you will all win _____ that say, 'I'm as fit as a/an

?

_____!' Good luck, class!"

★

From SPORTS STAR MAD LIBS JUNIOR® • Copyright © 2004 by Penguin Random House LLC.

MAD LIBS JUNIOR® is fun to play with friends, but you can also play it by yourself! To begin, look at the story on the page below. When you come to a blank space in the story, look at the symbol that appears underneath. Then find the same symbol on this page and pick a word that appears below the symbol. Put that word in the blank space, and cross out the word, so you don't use it again. Continue doing this throughout the story until you've filled in all the spaces. Finally, read your story aloud and laugh!

GYMNASTICS

★
NOUNS
clown
hippo
monkey
monster
watermelon
jellyfish
flamingo
elephant
alien
pickle
dinosaur
turtle

😊
ADJECTIVES
yucky
bad
silly
nasty
stinky
greasy
wild
wacky
skinny
goofy
slimy
slippery

➡
VERBS
tumble
dance
flip
burp
sing
fart
laugh
cheer
jump
twirl
roll
shake

?
MISC.
jumpsuit
leotard
ski mask
headband
glove
scarf
sweater
tutu
crown
mask
cape
eye patch

MAD LIBS ☺ JUNIOR.
GYMNASTICS

My little sister has been doing gymnastics for three years and can

_____ just like a/an _____. The other day, we

went to see her compete. She was wearing her lucky green

_____ that makes her look like a little _____.

Her first event was the uneven bars and she flipped around like a

_____ _____. When she finished, we all started

to _____. Her best event is the balance beam—a long,

_____ plank that's really tricky to balance on. When she's

on the beam, she's as graceful as a/an _____ on a high wire.

Her coach says that if she keeps up the _____ work,

she might make it to the Olympics one day!

From SPORTS STAR MAD LIBS JUNIOR® • Copyright © 2004 by Penguin Random House LLC.

MAD LIBS JUNIOR® is fun to play with friends, but you can also play it by yourself! To begin, look at the story on the page below. When you come to a blank space in the story, look at the symbol that appears underneath. Then find the same symbol on this page and pick a word that appears below the symbol. Put that word in the blank space, and cross out the word, so you don't use it again. Continue doing this throughout the story until you've filled in all the spaces. Finally, read your story aloud and laugh!

SURF DAD

★	😊	➡	?
NOUNS	**ADJECTIVES**	**VERBS**	**MISC.**
shark	snazzy	paddling	sunglasses
baby	crazy	screaming	water wings
turtle	silly	swimming	underwear
beach ball	nasty	crying	earrings
fish	funny	laughing	swim trunks
dolphin	fancy	snorting	shoes
kitten	cool	farting	boots
clam	awesome	splashing	goggles
starfish	stinky	yelling	pants
shrimp	stupid	floating	socks
sea lion	sad	bathing	flippers
whale	wild	giggling	gloves

MAD LIBS ☺ JUNIOR.
SURF DAD

Last summer, my family went on a/an _____ trip to Hawaii ☺

and my dad decided to learn how to surf. He rented a surfboard,

bought himself a/an _____ new pair of bright orange ☺

_____, and headed to the beach. The rest of us were **?**

_____ in the surf as he went out toward the big waves. It was **➡**

pretty _____! On his first try, he fell off the surfboard and ☺

started _____ like a _____. He had to be rescued **➡**   **★**

by a brave lifeguard, who dragged him out of the water by his

_____. But it was probably for the best, since we heard that **?**

later that day a surfer was attacked by a/an _____ ☺

_____! **★**

From SPORTS STAR MAD LIBS JUNIOR® • Copyright © 2004 by Penguin Random House LLC.

MAD LIBS JUNIOR® is fun to play with friends, but you can also play it by yourself! To begin, look at the story on the page below. When you come to a blank space in the story, look at the symbol that appears underneath. Then find the same symbol on this page and pick a word that appears below the symbol. Put that word in the blank space, and cross out the word, so you don't use it again. Continue doing this throughout the story until you've filled in all the spaces. Finally, read your story aloud and laugh!

SOCCER GAME

★	☺	→	?
NOUNS	**ADJECTIVES**	**VERBS**	**MISC.**
cupcakes	tough	crying	crown
toilets	mean	laughing	hat
ladybugs	nasty	burping	cape
losers	ugly	giggling	sweatshirt
monkeys	rough	whining	helmet
dump trucks	scary	farting	scarf
kittens	angry	cheering	cap
cream puffs	prickly	smiling	bathing suit
mice	yucky	screaming	sweat suit
clowns	creepy	singing	jersey
freaks	huge	weeping	jacket
toothpicks	evil	barfing	T-shirt

MAD LIBS JUNIOR.
SOCCER GAME

On Thursday, my soccer team had to play against a really

_____ team—the Fighting _____. Even their

coach is _____. She wears a big, _____

_____ that says, "There's No _____ in Soccer!"

When we scored a point, she started _____ and called the

referees "_____." Then there was this _____

player named Martha. When I got the ball, she came running toward me

and started _____. I was still able to kick the ball to one

of the other players, but started _____ as we scored a point.

But we were still _____! At halftime, our coach gave us a

big pep talk and said, "Go get 'em, _____!" Then we got

_____ and beat them 5-2!

From SPORTS STAR MAD LIBS JUNIOR® • Copyright © 2004 by Penguin Random House LLC.

MAD LIBS JUNIOR® is fun to play with friends, but you can also play it by yourself! To begin, look at the story on the page below. When you come to a blank space in the story, look at the symbol that appears underneath. Then find the same symbol on this page and pick a word that appears below the symbol. Put that word in the blank space, and cross out the word, so you don't use it again. Continue doing this throughout the story until you've filled in all the spaces. Finally, read your story aloud and laugh!

ICE HOCKEY

★ NOUNS	☺ ADJECTIVES	➡ VERBS	? MISC.
potatoes	silly	giggle	ice skates
daisies	old	fight	underwear
gum balls	funny	burp	goggles
ducks	awesome	laugh	slippers
bananas	cool	snort	masks
bottle caps	dumb	fart	helmets
pickles	friendly	wrestle	robes
peaches	dorky	skate	jerseys
turtles	tough	cry	mittens
boogers	wimpy	sing	jackets
turkeys	goofy	talk	earmuffs
butterflies	neat	dance	capes

Last weekend, my _____ aunt took me to see my very first

ice hockey game. I was so excited that I wanted to _____!

We went to see our local team, the _____ Penguins, who were

playing their rivals, the Yukon _____. The players on our team

were all wearing black _____ and big _____

?   ?

with penguins on them. I thought they looked really _____.

My aunt said that the object of hockey was to get as many

_____ into the goals as you could, but it seemed like all the

players did was _____. What a/an _____ game!

From SPORTS STAR MAD LIBS JUNIOR® • Copyright © 2004 by Penguin Random House LLC.

MAD LIBS JUNIOR® is fun to play with friends, but you can also play it by yourself! To begin, look at the story on the page below. When you come to a blank space in the story, look at the symbol that appears underneath. Then find the same symbol on this page and pick a word that appears below the symbol. Put that word in the blank space, and cross out the word, so you don't use it again. Continue doing this throughout the story until you've filled in all the spaces. Finally, read your story aloud and laugh!

MINI GOLF

★ NOUNS	☺ ADJECTIVES	→ VERBS	? MISC.
pizza	hairy	jump	knickers
puppies	lame	talk	sweaters
chicken wings	silly	giggle	gloves
nachos	bossy	snort	glasses
ponies	slimy	win	shoes
ice cream	chunky	boogie	pants
chips	ugly	bounce	vests
sodas	goofy	laugh	mittens
lollipops	lumpy	dance	slippers
trophies	crazy	roll	socks
balloons	smelly	sing	capes
French fries	wacky	fly	hats

MAD LIBS JUNIOR
MINI GOLF

My family loves to play mini golf, especially my _____ dad. My

mom always chooses a green ball, but my dad likes to find one that looks

really _____. "This one looks like it could _____,"

he always says with a big, _____ grin on his face. It's kind of

embarrassing because he wears funny plaid _____, like he's a

real golfer. He also screams, "_____!" every time he hits the

ball. Sometimes, he even pretends I'm his caddy and I have to carry around

his _____. Even though he's really _____, we

always let Dad win, because afterwards he buys us all _____

to celebrate!

From SPORTS STAR MAD LIBS JUNIOR® • Copyright © 2004 by Penguin Random House LLC.

MAD LIBS JUNIOR® is fun to play with friends, but you can also play it by yourself! To begin, look at the story on the page below. When you come to a blank space in the story, look at the symbol that appears underneath. Then find the same symbol on this page and pick a word that appears below the symbol. Put that word in the blank space, and cross out the word, so you don't use it again. Continue doing this throughout the story until you've filled in all the spaces. Finally, read your story aloud and laugh!

HOW TO DO A CARTWHEEL

★ NOUNS	😊 ADJECTIVES	➡ VERBS	? MISC.
starfish	slimy	laugh	sock
pancake	toothy	fart	underwear
octopus	dizzy	smile	shirt
marshmallow	pointy	burp	scarf
banana	cheap	grin	mitten
jellyfish	smelly	giggle	tie
yo-yo	fluffy	snort	bathing suit
butterfly	squishy	scream	mask
cupcake	hairy	grunt	cape
sunflower	greasy	howl	hat
scarecrow	ugly	yell	shoe
dolphin	nasty	groan	sweater

MAD LIBS JUNIOR.
HOW TO DO A CARTWHEEL

Learn the perfect way to do this _____ gymnastic move in

five simple steps:

Step 1: Tuck your _____ into your shorts, so it doesn't fall

over your _____ face when you flip over.

Step 2: Make sure you have a/an _____ surface to land on,

like a grassy patch or a/an _____ _____ .

Step 3: Spread your _____ feet apart and raise your arms

up, until you look like a/an _____ .

Step 4: Start to _____ slowly, then do it more quickly.

Soon, you'll feel yourself flipping like a/an _____ .

Step 5: Throw your arms and head back and give your audience a big

_____ .Ta da!

From SPORTS STAR MAD LIBS JUNIOR® • Copyright © 2004 by Penguin Random House LLC.

MAD LIBS JUNIOR® is fun to play with friends, but you can also play it by yourself! To begin, look at the story on the page below. When you come to a blank space in the story, look at the symbol that appears underneath. Then find the same symbol on this page and pick a word that appears below the symbol. Put that word in the blank space, and cross out the word, so you don't use it again. Continue doing this throughout the story until you've filled in all the spaces. Finally, read your story aloud and laugh!

TENNIS LESSONS

★ NOUNS	☺ ADJECTIVES	➡ VERBS	? MISC.
dinosaur	greasy	burp	socks
monkey	puffy	giggle	shorts
doll	slimy	move	sunglasses
turtle	fuzzy	wiggle	swim trunks
toilet	hot	laugh	overalls
bird	pretty	sing	sweat pants
robot	messy	fart	boots
alien	snotty	shake	mittens
horse	ugly	dance	pants
noodle	rich	snore	slippers
lizard	lazy	grunt	gloves
cupcake	dumb	sneeze	jeans

Last summer, my mom signed my _____ older sister and me

up for tennis lessons. Our instructor was a really _____

guy named Biff who looked just like a/an _____. He wore

_____ _____ ? and was always fixing his

_____ hair. I could tell that my sister had a crush on him,

because she would always _____ ➡ when he was around.

When it was really _____ outside he'd just sit around in

his _____ ?, drinking lemonade and bossing us around.

"Keep your eye on the _____ ★! Don't _____ ➡

so much while you're serving!" What a/an _____ ★

brain! Next summer, I hope we can just go to the pool!

From SPORTS STAR MAD LIBS JUNIOR® • Copyright © 2004 by Penguin Random House LLC.

MAD LIBS JUNIOR® is fun to play with friends, but you can also play it by yourself! To begin, look at the story on the page below. When you come to a blank space in the story, look at the symbol that appears underneath. Then find the same symbol on this page and pick a word that appears below the symbol. Put that word in the blank space, and cross out the word, so you don't use it again. Continue doing this throughout the story until you've filled in all the spaces. Finally, read your story aloud and laugh!

DIRT BIKE RACE

★	☺	→	?
NOUNS	**ADJECTIVES**	**VERBS**	**MISC.**
pumpkin	dangerous	explode	sock
wizard	wild	disappear	shirt
pirate	crazy	pop	crown
parrot	hairy	sing	helmet
dragon	stinky	fly	scarf
tree	cool	flip	mitten
trash can	smelly	float	shoe
toilet	scary	sparkle	T-shirt
octopus	slippery	growl	tie
pickle	ugly	dance	skirt
pogo stick	cheap	jump	hat
panther	rich	spin	belt

My _____ cousin Pete competes in dirt bike races. I love to

watch him _____ in the races. He always wears a

_____ on his head for safety, because dirt bikes can be very

_____ . Everyone calls him Pete the _____ ,

because one time he made his bike _____ in midair. Another

time during a race, he jumped his bike over a/an _____

in the middle of the dirt bike track. He gets extra points for doing

_____ tricks, so he's always trying something. He just

won a race the other day and got a big trophy shaped like a/an

_____ and a check for one hundred dollars.

From SPORTS STAR MAD LIBS JUNIOR® • Copyright © 2004 by Penguin Random House LLC.

MAD LIBS JUNIOR® is fun to play with friends, but you can also play it by yourself! To begin, look at the story on the page below. When you come to a blank space in the story, look at the symbol that appears underneath. Then find the same symbol on this page and pick a word that appears below the symbol. Put that word in the blank space, and cross out the word, so you don't use it again. Continue doing this throughout the story until you've filled in all the spaces. Finally, read your story aloud and laugh!

AT THE BALLPARK

★ NOUNS	☺ ADJECTIVES	→ VERBS	? MISC.
pickles	best	shakes	socks
rubber bands	worst	dances	caps
sardines	coolest	farts	shirts
peanuts	hottest	sings	shorts
lightbulbs	slimiest	laughs	jerseys
onions	greasiest	burps	gloves
hot dogs	greatest	claps	shoes
chickens	nastiest	cheers	ties
marshmallows	tastiest	jumps	hats
insects	smelliest	wiggles	boots
noodles	silliest	barfs	slippers
French fries	ugliest	sways	belts

MAD LIBS JUNIOR.
AT THE BATTING CAGE

The other night, my family went to _____ some baseballs

at the batting cage. I was so excited, I wore my favorite _____.

?

My parents said I could hit first, since I'm the _____ kid in

the family. I went up to bat and fixed my _____ just right and

?

got ready to swing. The first ball went whizzing past my head like a

speeding _____. I swung a _____ at the ball

really hard, but I missed and my _____ went flying off. Then

?

I grabbed the _____ bat I could find. When the next ball

came, I gave it a big _____ and sent it flying. I felt like the

_____ kid in the world!

From SPORTS STAR MAD LIBS JUNIOR® • Copyright © 2004 by Penguin Random House LLC.

MAD LIBS JUNIOR® is fun to play with friends, but you can also play it by yourself! To begin, look at the story on the page below. When you come to a blank space in the story, look at the symbol that appears underneath. Then find the same symbol on this page and pick a word that appears below the symbol. Put that word in the blank space, and cross out the word, so you don't use it again. Continue doing this throughout the story until you've filled in all the spaces. Finally, read your story aloud and laugh!

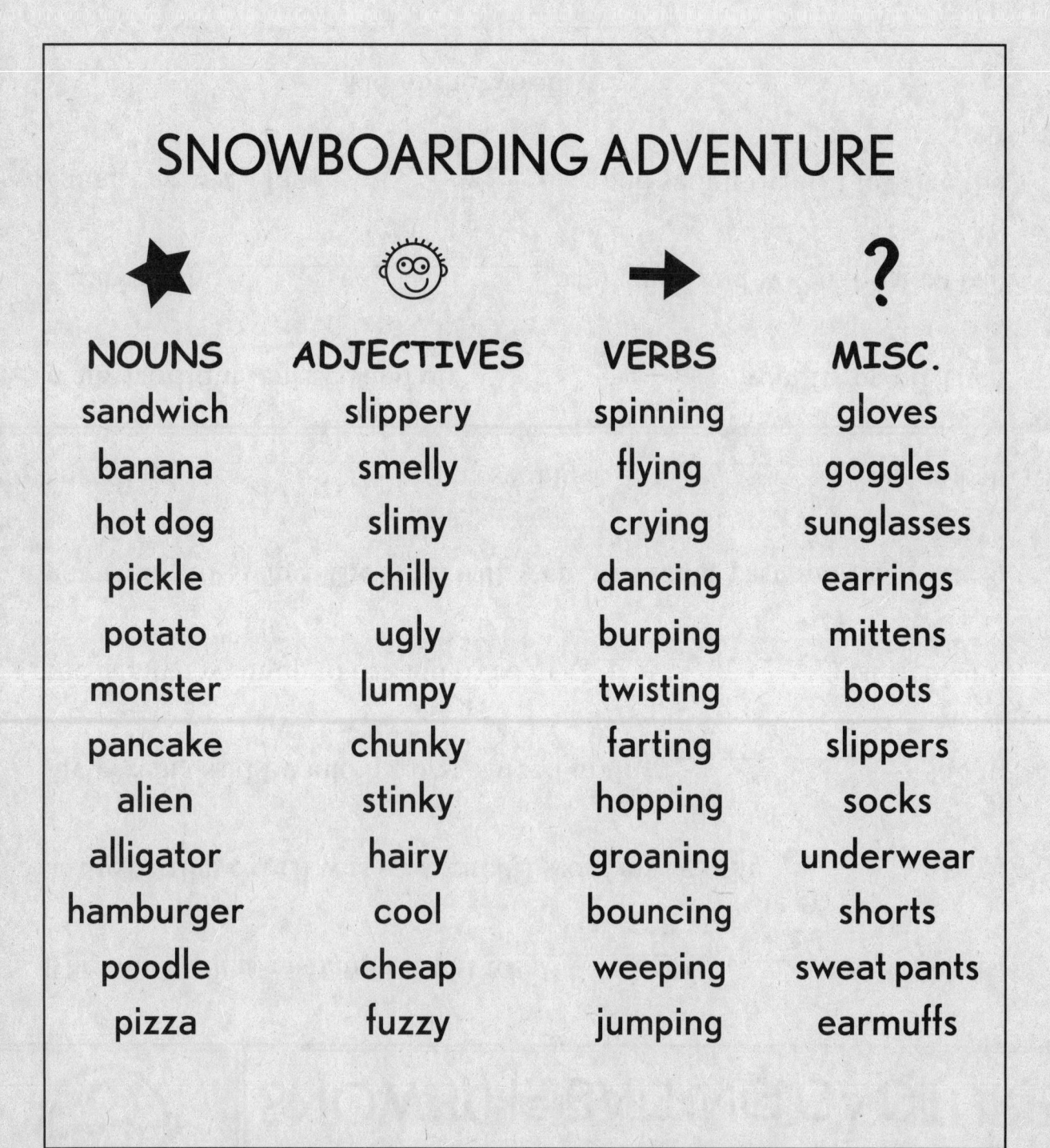

SNOWBOARDING ADVENTURE

★ NOUNS	😀 ADJECTIVES	→ VERBS	? MISC.
sandwich	slippery	spinning	gloves
banana	smelly	flying	goggles
hot dog	slimy	crying	sunglasses
pickle	chilly	dancing	earrings
potato	ugly	burping	mittens
monster	lumpy	twisting	boots
pancake	chunky	farting	slippers
alien	stinky	hopping	socks
alligator	hairy	groaning	underwear
hamburger	cool	bouncing	shorts
poodle	cheap	weeping	sweat pants
pizza	fuzzy	jumping	earmuffs

MAD LIBS JUNIOR.
SNOWBOARDING ADVENTURE

This winter, my family went skiing on the _____ slopes of

the Colorado Rockies. I took my new _____ snowboard

that my _____ uncle had given me. A snowboard looks

kind of like a big, flat _____ and you ride it like a

surfboard. The first day of our trip, I threw on the _____

new _____ my mom had bought me and hit the slopes.

On my first run, my board started _____ and I fell all the

way down the mountain. When I got up, I looked like a snow-covered

_____ . I found my _____ in a tree. Then I saw

that my thumb looked like a swollen _____ . I was so

upset, I started _____ right there in the snow.

From SPORTS STAR MAD LIBS JUNIOR® • Copyright © 2004 by Penguin Random House LLC.

Download Mad Libs today!

Join the millions of Mad Libs fans
creating wacky and wonderful
stories on our apps!